The World of Color

Green in My World

by Joanne Winne

Welcome
Books

Children's Press
A Division of Grolier Publishing
New York / London / Hong Kong / Sydney
Danbury, Connecticut

Photo Credits: Cover and all photos by Thaddeus Harden
Contributing Editors: Mark Beyer and Magdalena Alagna
Book Design: Michael DeLisio

Visit Children's Press on the Internet at:
http://publishing.grolier.com

Library of Congress Cataloging-in-Publication Data

Winne, Joanne.
    Green in my world / by Joanne Winne.
    p. cm. — (The world of color)
    Includes bibliographical references and index.
    Summary: A simple story highlights such green things as green grass, green trees,
and salad.
    ISBN 0-516-23124-3 (lib. bdg.) — ISBN 0-516-23049-2 (pbk.)
    1. Green—Juvenile literature. [1. Green. 2. Color.] I. Title.

QC495.5.W5644 2000
535.6—dc21

                                                                        00-024365

Contents

My name is Tim.

This is my **backyard**.

What do you see in my yard that is green?

5

The trees and grass are green.

The **hose** and **rake** are green, too.

My friends and I play by the **creek**.

Plants grow beside the creek.

Can you name the green plants?

9

The green plant on the
rocks is **moss**.

The plant with leaves is a
fern.

Moss and ferns grow in the
shade.

10

11

Many animals live by the creek.

What is this green animal called?

13

This animal is a frog.

Many frogs are green.

Frogs make good pets.

15

I help to make dinner.

I'm making a **salad**.

How many of the foods that you see are green?

17

There are three green foods.

Lettuce and **spinach** are green.

Cucumber is green, too.

19

Green can be found everywhere.

What do you see around you that is green?

21

New Words

backyard (bak-**yard**) place behind a house
creek (**kreek**) a small river
cucumber (**kyoo**-kum-ber) a green crunchy
    vegetable
fern (**fern**) a plant with small leaves that grows in
    the shade
hose (**hohz**) a tube that water comes out of
lettuce (**let**-is) a light green food
moss (**maws**) a light green plant that grows on
    rocks or parts of trees
rake (**rayk**) a tool that is used in a garden
salad (**sal**-id) a meal made from lettuce or
    spinach
shade (**shayd**) a place where the sun is blocked
spinach (**spin**-ich) a dark green food

To Find Out More

Book

Orchard's Little Green Book of Nursery Rhymes
by Nila Aye
Orchard Books

Web Site

Crayola
www.crayola.com
This is the official Crayola Web site. It has a lot
of pictures to print and color. It also has craft
ideas, games, and online art.

Index

About the Author
Joanne Winne taught fourth grade for nine years. She currently writes and edits books for children. She lives in Hoboken, New Jersey.

Reading Consultants
Kris Flynn, Coordinator, Small School District Literacy, The San Diego County Office of Education

Shelly Forys, Certified Reading Recovery Specialist, W.J. Zahnow Elementary School, Waterloo, IL

Peggy McNamara, Professor, Bank Street College of Education, Reading and Literacy Program